gudetama™

love for
the lazy

SIL-34865

written and illustrated by
wook-jin clark

Color flats by Jason Fisher
Lettered by Tom B. Long
with additional hand lettering by Wook-Jin Clark

Edited by Sarah Gaydos
Designed by Kate Z. Stone

gudetama™

love for
the lazy

Withdrawn

USED UNDER LICENSE SANRIO INC

Sanrio

USA

SIL-34865

Published by Oni-Lion Forge Publishing Group, LLC

James Lucas Jones, president & publisher • Sarah Gaydos, editor in chief
Charlie Chu, e.v.p. of creative & business development • Brad Rooks, director of operations
Amber O'Neill, special projects manager • Harris Fish, events manager
Margot Wood, director of marketing & sales • Jeremy Atkins, director of brand communications
Devin Funches, sales & marketing manager • Katie Sainz, marketing manager
Tara Lehmann, marketing & publicity associate • Troy Look, director of design & production
Kate Z. Stone, senior graphic designer • Sonja Synak, graphic designer
Hilary Thompson, graphic designer • Sarah Rockwell, junior graphic designer
Angie Knowles, digital prepress lead • Vincent Kukua, digital prepress technician
Shawna Gore, senior editor • Robin Herrera, senior editor • Amanda Meadows, senior editor
Jasmine Amiri, editor • Grace Bornhoft, editor • Zack Soto, editor • Steve Ellis, vice president of games
Ben Eisner, game developer • Michelle Nguyen, executive assistant • Jung Lee, logistics coordinator

Joe Nozemack, publisher emeritus

1319 SE Martin Luther King, Jr. Blvd.
Suite 240
Portland, OR 97214

onipress.com   **lionforge.com**
facebook.com/onipress   facebook.com/lionforge
twitter.com/onipress   twitter.com/lionforge
instagram.com/onipress   instagram.com/lionforge

**instagram.com/gudetama/
twitter.com/gudetamatweets
sanrio.com**

**twitter.com/wookjinclark
wookjinclark.com**

gudetama™
by Sanrio®

©2013, 2019 SANRIO CO., LTD.
Used Under License.
www.sanrio.com

SIL-34865

First Edition: January 2020

Retail ISBN 978-1-62010-728-7
Oni Exclusive Variant ISBN 978-1-62010-771-3
eISBN 978-1-62010-729-4

1 2 3 4 5 6 7 8 9 10

Library of Congress Control Number
2019952616

Printed in USA.

**Retail Cover by Wook-Jin Clark
Oni Exclusive Variant Cover by Derek Charm**

BZZZ

BZZZ
BZZZ

NEW PHONE, WHO DIS?

9:21AM 71%

CARMELO

HI, GUDETAMA, MY NAME'S CARMELO! I WANNA MEET SOMEONE IRL, NOT ON AN APP. I JUST WANT SPONTANEITY! CAN YOU HELP ME?

...WELL, I GUESS...

I'VE TRIED MEETING PEOPLE AT THE LIBRARY, ON THE TRAIN, AT COFFEE SHOPS, PRETTY MUCH EVERYWHERE, BUT EACH TIME I JUST REPEL PEOPLE. I DON'T KNOW WHAT MY PROBLEM IS! HELP!!

WHAT AM I DOING WRONG? HELP ME, GUDETAMA!

...I CAN TRY...

SO, I REALLY NEED YOUR HELP WI--

DING

...ANYWAYS, SO, I REALLY NE--

DING

ARE YOU GOOD? I CAN ALWAYS...

IT'S NOTHING... KEEP GOING.

OKAY, WELL, SO I HAVE THIS THI--

DING

DO YOU NEED TO GET THAT? IT SEEMS LIKE SOMEONE IS REALLY TRYING TO REACH YOU.

IT'S NOT IMPORTANT.

IT'S JUST PEOPLE MESSAGING ME ON *LURVER*. YOU KNOW, THAT DATING APP.

WHOA!

hi ;)

25 NEW messages!

HOW ARE YOU GETTING ALL THESE MESSAGES?

THIS IS TOTALLY WHY I NEED YOUR HELP...I NEVER GET *ANY!*

HI! I'M CARSON.

I WAS BORN ON A COLD, RAINY NIGHT IN 1992. IT WAS A TUESDAY.

I HAVE A THIRD NIPPLE.

MY FRECKLES TELL SECRET MESSAGES. MESSAGES THAT THE APOCALYPSE IS NEAR!

SO LET'S GO ON A DATE, SINCE THE WORLD MIGHT BE ENDING.

... SOMETIMES, LESS IS MORE.

TO BE FAIR, GUDETAMA ALSO FELL ASLEEP HALFWAY THROUGH FILLING OUT THEIR PROFILE.

WE ALL HAVE DIFFERENT PRIORITIES...

end.

I THINK SOMEONE LIKES ME, GUDETAMA! THEY KEEP GLANCING OVER...

ARE THEY INTO ME?

FIRST, LOOK BEHIND YOU AND MAKE SURE THERE'S NO ONE ELSE AROUND.

? ?

SECOND, STAND BEHIND YOUR HOTTEST FRIEND AND SEE IF THEIR GAZE FOLLOWS YOU.

? ? ?

THIRD, LOCATE THE SUN'S POSITION AND NOTE THE TIME OF DAY.

DRAW A SIGHT LINE FROM YOU TO THEM, AND IF THE RATIO AND ANGLE IS GREATER THAN X, YOU'RE GOOD.

$$\frac{z\sqrt{4x}}{7D}$$

IF ALL 3 REQUIREMENTS ARE MET, YOU CAN NOW GO TO PHASE 2.

WHAT'S PHASE 2?

ONE QUESTION PER PERSON.

end.

IT'S SIMPLE, REALLY. SET THEIR EXPECTATIONS LOW.

JUST MAKE THE FIRST DATE GOOD ENOUGH.

IT CAN ONLY GO UP FROM THERE.

UHHH...

YEAHHH, I CAN'T DO THAT.

YOU'RE NOT GIVING ME ANYTHING I CAN ACTUALLY USE!

HEY, YOU DIDN'T SAY THE ANSWER HAD TO BE RIGHT!

end.

UGH...LET ME CHECK MY EMAIL. SO MANY OF YOU NEED ADVICE, BUT I JUST WOKE UP...

GUDETAMA, *HALP!* I'M AN O.J. PERSON, AND MY PARTNER IS A CRANBERRY JUICE PERSON. EVERY BRUNCH ENDS IN TEARS!

HMM...

WELL, I SEE THREE OPTIONS...

BREAK UP.

NO!

SWITCH TO CRANBERRY AND BE UNHAPPY FOREVER..

NO! NO!

MYSTERY OPTION.

...

I-I GUESS I'LL DO OPTION THREE.

WHAT DO I DO?

SHA!

♥ MIX BOTH DRINKS.

THEY SEEM LIKE SUCH A GREAT MATCH FOR YOU...THEY'RE *BOTH* INTO GAMES!

I KNOW! THEY BOTH SEEM AWESOME...

BUT I'M SO ANXIOUS, I KNOW I'LL MESS IT UP...AND I CAN'T EVEN CHOOSE WHICH ONE TO GO OUT WITH!

CAN'T I JUST STAY HOME?!

UGH... FINE.

LET'S MAKE YOUR DATE FEEL LIKE A GAME. MAYBE THAT WILL HELP EASE YOUR ANXIETY.

BUT I STILL DON'T KNOW WHO TO CHOOSE!

YOU'LL NEVER MEET SOMEONE IF YOU DON'T AT LEAST GIVE IT A TRY.

GUDETAMA, A LITTLE HELP?

PROBLEM SOLVED...

wook jin clark

was born in South Korea and raised in South Carolina. He loves coffee, doodling, walking around, and COFFEE!! Look for his work in Image Comic's *Flavor*, Boom's *Bee and Puppycat*, *Regular Show*, *Adventure Time*, and *Bravest Warriors* comics.

making of

gudetama™

love for the lazy

by Wook-Jin Clark

It all starts out with a script!

Panel 1: *Close up on Gudetama. Not facing us. We just see its butt.*

Gudetama: Argh...

Panel 2: *Gudetama turns around.*

Gudetama: Oh, hey...
Gudetama: I'm Gudetama.

Panel 3: *Same panel as previous, but there is a pair of toes dancing through in the foreground.*

Gudetama: ...

Panel 4: *Pull out to show Nisetama.*

Nisetama: And I'm Gudetama's buddy, Nisetama!
Nisetama: We're here to help people looking for love!

Panel 5: *Close up on Gudetama who is unenthusiastic.*

Gudetama: Yeahhh...What he said...
Gudetama: But first, a little nap?

Nisetama pulls the bottom of the page corner fold to start the book.

Nisetama: But Gudetama, everyone needs us!
Nisetama: C'mon! Let's go!

And then on to pencils!

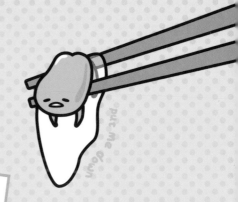

Next up, I ink the pages.

And finally, they are colored & lettered!

read more from oni press!